# Throw Jezebel Down

## *"Renouncing alliances and associations with the spirit of Jezebel"*

---

## By: Robert Summers

**Published by**
**Summers Ministries**
**Columbus, Ohio**

Printed in USA

*And when Jehu was come to Jezreel, Jezebel heard of it; and she painted her face, and tired her head, and looked out at a window. And as Jehu entered in at the gate, she said, Had Zimri peace, who slew his master? And he lifted up his face to the window, and said, Who is on my side? who? And there looked out to him two or three eunuchs. And he said, **Throw her down**. So they threw her down: and some of her blood was sprinkled on the wall, and on the horses: and he trode her under foot. And when he was come in, he did eat and drink, and said, Go, see now this cursed woman, and bury her: for she is a king's daughter. And they went to bury her: but they found no more of her than the skull, and the feet, and the palms of her hands?*

*2 Kings 9:30-35 New James Version*

# Table of Contents

Introduction

# Introduction

Jezebel is an evil ancient spirit that has been causing havoc in families, marriages, business, churches and individuals for thousands of years. It is a spirit that is undaunted in securing her stronghold in the souls of men and women everywhere even when her malicious tactics are deployed in plain sight. Jezebel secures access through the flesh. Whether it's through the un-crucified nature of an unbeliever or the carnal mindset of a believer, Jezebel is an equal opportunity demonic spirit. She preys on the simple minded and defenseless. She attacks every race, gender and nation. Among her preferred targets are innocent children, wounded women, and male leaders. She will exploit every opportunity given to her and is a master tactician at controlling lives.

Today, there is an abundance of teaching on the topic of Jezebel. Much of it is good. Some of it is - not so good. Every student of the word of God should, at the very least, have a high-level teaching on the topic of Spiritual Warfare, and the Jezebel spirit in particular. However, the purpose of this resource is not to educate one in the characteristics, traits and inter-workings of the Jezebel spirit. Rather, its purpose is to provide leverage to those affected by Jezebel's witchcrafts, and support them in their journey of gaining freedom from Jezebel's web of destruction.

Without question Jezebel desires to influence your life in every capacity insomuch that you will never achieve any measurable peace. When afflicted by Jezebel, your peace is stolen and your life is miserable.

*And it came to pass, when Joram saw Jehu, that he said, Is it peace, Jehu? And he answered, What peace, so long as the whoredoms of thy mother Jezebel and her witchcrafts are so many – II Kings 9:22*

It doesn't take the anointing of Elijah to root Jezebel out of your life. It takes a citizen of the Kingdom of Heaven that understands their rights to simply say -**"No More!"** No more will you tolerate her witchcrafts. No more will you tolerate her influence, abuse, control, manipulation and sorcery.

Christ has set you free from the power of darkness. Satan, demons nor the spirit of Jezebel has any power over you. Consider the following scriptures that articulate Christ's victory over the kingdom of darkness:

*And having spoiled principalities and powers, he made a shew of them openly, triumphing over them in it - Colossians 2:15*

*Forasmuch then as the children are partakers of flesh and blood, he also himself likewise took part of the same;*

*that through death he might destroy him that had the power of death, that is, the devil – Hebrews 2:14*

*And he said unto them, I beheld Satan as lightning fall from heaven. – Luke 10:18*

*For this purpose the Son of God was manifested, that he might destroy the works of the devil. – I John 3:8(b)*

*And the devil that deceived them was cast into the lake of fire and brimstone, where the beast and the false prophet are, and shall be tormented day and night for ever and ever – Revelation 20:10*

You can plainly see that the devil or any of his demonic host, including Jezebel cannot overpower a believer. However, the enemy can deceive a believer.

*Put on the whole armour of God, that ye may be able to stand against the wiles of the devil. – Ephesians 6:11*

The Greek word for 'wiles' is *"Methodeia"* Meaning - methods, cunning arts, deceit, craft and trickery.

Our battle is not against the devil himself, but rather our battle is against the deception of the devil. This is precisely how Jezebel navigates her way into churches, families, business and individual's lives - through deception!

Jezebel is a master at disguising herself. Her greatest asset is to remain hidden. She is phenomenal at blending in and remaining undetected by most people. She is like a chameleon in the spirit. Her highly developed ability to appear one way yet operate in a completely different manner causes a whirlwind of strife, confusion and havoc. Jezebel initially comes across as the innocent bystander. Many times she plays the role of a victim of others. This is designed to weaken her intended prey.

As you probably know by now, Jezebel has perfected the art of lying. This spirit can manipulate the host and its victims and make them believe up is down, and right is left. She is notorious for hypnotizing her prey through a manipulative tactic called false compassion. She will make you feel she's for you, and no one else understands you like she does. This could operate through a friend, a church leader or family member. Jezebelic Mothers will use false compassion as a means to control her children. Remember, Jezebel's ultimate goal is to gain control over your life.

Again, most of Jezebels tactics are performed in a covert manner. As long as Jezebel gets her way, she's fine and will remain under the radar screen. However her chameleon like style is nothing more than a painted face that will have you embracing her treacherous ways.

*And when Jehu was come to Jezreel, Jezebel heard of it; and she painted her face, and tired her head, and looked out at a window – II Kings 9:30*

The painting of Jezebel's face was something more than a fashion statement. For a queen, it was a way of displaying her rank as a higher power. Jezebel takes pride in her masterful ability to deceive her host and victims. It is her way of flexing muscle and letting you [and others] know she is in charge.

Let's face it, your encounters and subsequent bondage with the Jezebel spirit did not occur overnight. Jezebel picks at your life little by little. If she can find one crack in your life, she will expose it and capitalize on the opportunity to seduce you into her bedchamber to perform her commands, or, aggressively assault you thus rendering you weak, timid and depressed.

Jezebel embeds herself effortlessly in those that came from a dysfunctional family. Families that have a history of addictions (drugs, alcoholism, tobacco, foods), sexual perversions and promiscuity, mental illnesses, poverty, depression, laziness, abuse (verbal, emotional, physical, sexual) and parental domination – attract Jezebel to them. Additionally, those that carry deep hurts and wounds from the past, and are unforgiving and bitter become magnets for this ghastly spirit to latch on to. Because this occurs over a period of time, the spirit of Jezebel creates a fortified place in your mind called a stronghold. This stronghold lodges deep within your subconscious (heart). Everything you do or say comes from the programming that exists in your subconscious. Jezebel creates a delusion or false-identity of yourself. Internally you view yourself in a manner that is not conducive with what the word of God says about you. Externally, your view of others and the world around you is perverted. With that type of mind-set you end up miserable, frustrated and never achieve your true destiny in life.

To keep you bound for life, Jezebel will keep you active. Perhaps she will lead you down a path of some form of 'success'. However, activity or movement alone means nothing if you're headed in the wrong direction. And success in the wrong thing is a catastrophe that steals your time, relationships and Kingdom purpose. This is called being entangled in her web of destruction.

### Breaking free

To liberate your-self from Jezebel is not as difficult as some make it out to be. I've read many publications that give you all the steps, formulas and ways to tackle this ancient spirit. But at the end of the day, after all the fasting and shouting, after the countless prayer lines to have hands laid on you and the numerous ounces of oil poured on you, it all comes down to this - **STOP TOLERATING JEZEBEL!!!!!**

*Nevertheless, I have this against you: <u>You tolerate</u> that woman Jezebel ...... Revelation 2:20 (NIV)*

The Jezebel spirit has power simply because you have tolerated it. As a born-again believer you are a citizen in the Kingdom of Heaven. As such, you have full rights, privileges and benefits of the Kingdom. This is why understanding the Kingdom must be your first priority! Without a significant comprehension of the governing authority of the Kingdom of Heaven ruling in your life, you will never truly realize the authority you have to contend with evil.

Your authority as a believer is because you are a citizen of Heaven. With Jezebel it's a constant battle for people in authority, specifically believers. As long as you are in authority you will run into this spirit. So, what do you need to do? **CONTEND WITH JEZEBEL!!!!**

Jezebel needs to learn the meaning of the word - **NO!** This book is designed to assist you in saying **No.** Whether through declarations, decrees, binding, rebuking or renouncing, it's time to come out of agreement with the spirit of Jezebel and reverse the affects of her vicious attacks.

Start now by verbally saying out loud, "I will no longer tolerate the spirit of Jezebel from operating in or through my life." Say it again; emphatically, **"I will no longer tolerate the spirit of Jezebel from operating in or through my life!"**

Glory to God, Jezebel's days are over.

**Prayer from Apostle Summers:**

"Father, it is my prayer that every person who reads this book and submits their mind, will, emotion and life to the government of the Kingdom and Lordship of Jesus Christ will start their journey on the path of deliverance.

Jezebel, you are defeated (Rev 2:22-23; 20:10, 2 Kings 9:33). Jezebel, you're not a queen, you are a witch. You are not a virgin, you are a whore. Every altar of witchcraft and idolatry erected in the lives of those reading this book will be destroyed as they engage in these renunciations. You no longer rule their life. Every assignment against them, their family, their ministry, their children, business and church are being canceled out, in Jesus name.

I agree that as they confess these renunciations, decrees and rebukes that they become emancipated, delivered and set-free from the sprit of Jezebel. I pray healing for their bodies and restoration of their soul. I pray that as they boldly confess their faith and trust in you Jesus, that every demonic cord, every tie that binds and every fetter that locks them is broken, in Jesus name.

Father, I pray restoration for families and marriages in the name of Jesus. I declare freedom; deliverance, healing, joy, peace and prosperity for all that pray these prayers. Lord, release your arrow of deliverance into their life. Repair the breach and let the light of your word expose every area of darkness. Let every demonic cave be sealed and every fiery dart be extinguished.

Father, I acknowledge that your Word rules and reigns over their mind and therefore they are stable in their soul. I thank you Father, for their complete deliverance and breakthrough in Jesus name. - Walk in victory"

## Declarations, Decrees and Commands

In the Bible, the word **declare** originates from the Hebrew word *'achvah'*, meaning, "to make known". It is speaking about publicly revealing or bringing something into the open. It can be likened to Customs Services located in airports. Custom agents may ask international travelers, "Do you have anything to declare?" What they are asking is "do you want to make something known to us."

Synonyms for the word decree is, proclaim, announce, state, and reveal, air, voice, articulate and express.

Spiritual declarations are what we speak out loud to make known what we already possess, presently desire or expect to occur in the future. They also reveal anything that is hiding in the darkness.

In contrast, a **decree** is an official order given by a person with power or by a government. Decrees are forceful decisions made by someone that is in or has the authority to act. When a decree is spoken or written by the one that is in authority or power, it becomes law.

Synonyms for the word decree is, command, dictate, direct, mandate, ordain, order and call.

It is important for believers to declare, decree and command their freedom from Jezebel's witchcrafts. It is in the nature of every born-again believer to call things that are not as though they were.

*(As it is written, I have made thee a father of many nations,) before him whom he believed, even God, who quickeneth the dead, and calleth those things which be not as though they were* – Romans 4:17

In Hebrew, decree means, *"to divide, separate and destroy."* This definition reveals what happens in the spiritual realm to Jezebels network and power operating in your life when you decree a thing.

*Thou shalt also decree a thing, and it shall be established unto thee: and the light shall shine upon thy ways* - Job 22:28

Finally, **command** is the Greek word *"paraggellō"* and it means to transmit a message, to charge, to declare (or) to announce.

The Merriam-Webster dictionary defines command as:

To give (someone) an order: to tell (someone) to do something in a forceful and often official way: to have authority and control over (a group of people, such as soldiers).

In the book of Acts, we see Paul commanding the spirit of divination to come out of a slave girl.

Paul and Silas were preaching the word of God and ministering when a damsel possessed with a spirit of witchcraft started following them and proclaiming, *"These men are the servants of the Most High God, who proclaim to us the way of salvation"* (Acts 16:17).

This girl would follow Paul and Silas around and announce to the entire city that they were sent from God. She was proclaiming the truth, however the spirit of Jezebel (witchcraft) motivated her. She was actually hindering the work of God and became a distraction. The Bible says she did this for many days before Paul finally commanded the devil to come out of her.

*And it came to pass, as we went to prayer, a certain damsel possessed with a spirit of divination met us, which brought her masters much gain by soothsaying: The same followed Paul and us, and cried, saying, These men are the servants of the most high God, which shew unto us the way of salvation. And this did she many days. But Paul, being grieved, turned and said to the spirit, I command thee in the name of Jesus Christ to come out of her. And he came out the same hour – Acts 16:16-18*

Declarations, decrees and commands are actions of faith. Faith can move mountains. Mountains represent obstacles that stand in your way and keep you from knowing your true purpose in life and ultimate destiny.

Begin now to use the authority that you have as a believer to *"tread on serpents and scorpions"* (Luke 10:19) and over all the false power [authority] of Jezebel.

---

I declare emancipation and independence from Satan, all evil spirits, demons and the dark powers of the underworld.

I declare emancipation from the spirit of Jezebel and her network of false prophetic gifts, operations, administration, words, songs, dances and artifacts.

I declare myself liberated from religion, tradition, racism, legalism, spiritual foolishness, heresy, vain imaginations, false offerings, false tithes, false seed, false deliverance, false healings, lying spirits and lying dreams – all tied to Jezebel.

I declare that light has come to my mind and emotions. And that darkness can no longer dwell in my mind, or body. (Eph 5:10-11)

I declare every Jezebelic scheme, plan, and plot against my life, my family, my land and my property be exposed now, in the name of Jesus.

I declare a divorce with the spirit of Jezebel and my immediate termination of all Jezebelic [idol] worship that she ever received through my ignorance of her devises.

I declare, decree and nullify any and every covenant I ever made with Jezebel, knowingly or unknowingly.

I declare that the throne of Jezebel's false authority will not be established in my life and that I will worship God and Him only.

I declare that I am coming into the fullness of my citizenship in the Kingdom of God. Therefore Jezebel has no authority, power or control over my life.

I declare that I am an overcomer and that I am empowered to defeat the witch known as Jezebel.

I declare that the plans of Jezebel are crushed like stoneware into tiny fragments.

I declare my inheritance, which is to have children and to enjoy fellowship with them.

I declare that Jezebel's plans and plots against my life are in continual state of chaos and never come to fruition.

I declare that Jezebel's manipulation tactics will not achieve any results in my life.

I declare peace over my life, my children and my house in Jesus' name.

I declare myself liberated from Jezebels stronghold of fear, torment and intimidation.

I declare all spirits of Jezebel operating in my family and marriage to be removed.

I decree freedom from the dark underworld of Jezebel's kingdom.

I decree emancipation from false apostolic authority, false prophetic words, witchcraft prayers, false covering, charismatic sorcerers, false fathers, counterfeits, fakes, phonies, players, haters, manipulators, religious generals, soul ties to Bishops, prophetic spiritualists and lying legalism.

I decree that the fire of God (judgment) is destroying all the works of Jezebel.

I decree that because I have exposed Jezebel and removed her from my life that I receive power over the nations (Rev. 2:26).

I decree torment, distress and emptiness is Jezebel's portion.

I decree plagues of loss, sorrow, dearth and famine is Jezebel's portion.

I decree upon Jezebel and her network spiritual confusion, deafness, dumbness, blindness, incapacitation and paralysis.

I decree the judgment of destruction upon the unrepentant spirit of Jezebel.

I command Jezebel's eunuchs' to disconnect from her bewitchments.

I command Jezebel's eunuchs' to throw her out of her place of authority.

I command the hounds (persecution) be released against Jezebel, her witchcrafts and whoredoms (1 Kings 21:23).

I command every mask, veil, covering and every hiding place of Jezebel in m y life be exposed.

I command Jezebel, to release and let go of all my resources including land, property, animals, jewelry, investments, money and the finances of people who owe me money.

# Rebukes

*Yet Michael the archangel, when contending with the devil he disputed about the body of Moses, durst not bring against him a railing accusation, but said, The Lord <u>rebuke</u> thee* – Jude 1:9

To **rebuke** means to reprimand; strongly warn; or restrain. It also means to contend with. Other words associated with rebuke include; chide, reprimand, reproach, reprove, denounce and put down.

The Webster's Revised Unabridged Dictionary states that Rebuke is to; check, silence, or put down, with reproof; to restrain by expression of disapprobation; to reprehend sharply, to chide; to reprove; to admonish. It is a direct and pointed reproof; a reprimand; chastisement or punishment.

Believers are to contend with the witchcrafts of Jezebel. Contend is to challenge. We must never tolerate the spirit of Jezebel in our life, our churches, families or nation. Jezebel and her activities must be put-down with strong and sharp rebukes. Kingdom citizens have the authority to rebuke Jezebel in Jesus name.

As a child of God and citizen of His Kingdom you have a covenant right to be free from Jezebels enslavement. Boldly rebuking Jezebel with authority puts her on notice that you are exposing her evil network to the full power of God Almighty.

---

I rebuke and cut off the spirit of whoredoms (Hos. 4:12).

I rebuke and cut off Jezebel and her witchcrafts in the name of Jesus (2 Kings 9:22).

I rebuke the spirit of Jezebel and break her power in my marriage.

I rebuke the spirit of Herodias and break every form of retaliation against my family, my ministry and me.

I rebuke the spirits of witchcraft, lust, seduction, intimidation, idolatry, and whoredom connected to Jezebel.

I rebuke and server all ties with Jezebel 'the whore of witchcrafts' and break her power over my life, my family and my nation (Nahum. 3:4).

I rebuke the spirit of harlotry and break it's power from over my life and family (Nahum 3:4).

I rebuke all spirits of false teaching, false prophecy, idolatry, perversion and immorality connected with Jezebel (Rev. 2:20).

I rebuke all spirits of false doctrine, false laying on of hands, false compassion and false authority connected to Jezebel.

I rebuke the spirit of control that binds me to Jezebelic women.

I rebuke maternal control off every dimension of my life in Jesus name.

I rebuke the spirit of rejection, un-forgiveness and bitterness from operating in my life due to a stronghold of hurt and abuse.

I rebuke and uproot every word curse released by Jezebel against my life.

I rebuke every Jezebelic seed (spirit of Athaliah) that looks to kill my seed, posterity and legacy.

I rebuke all retaliatory spirits released through Jezebel's fury, rage, anger, hatred, and intimidation against my body, my spine, my brain, my glands, (specifically the pineal gland), and every organ in my body, cells, bones, bone marrow, muscles, and tissue.

I rebuke Jezebel's witchcraft released against me through prayers of witchcraft, voodoo, Christian word curses, prophetic sorcery, divination, and chants.

I rebuke, uproot, saw asunder, cast down, overthrow, destroy, and pulverize all of Jezebel's witchcraft, whoredoms and perversion against me through the wickedness of clergy, men of the cloth, Bishops, Bishop-Elects, Ministers, Pastors, Apostles, Prophets, Evangelists, Teachers (including Sunday school teachers), Superintendents, Overseers, Elders, First Ladies, Worship leaders, Administrators, Praise dancers and Deacons.

I rebuke all thoughts of quitting my ministry, my business, my spouse, my family, my life or abandoning God.

I rebuke suicidal thoughts, depression and heaviness of heart.

I rebuke all sexually impure thoughts of pornography, adultery, masturbation, homosexuality and fornication.

I rebuke the effects of any sexual or emotional abuses against me as a child, including (and within the marriage covenant) sexual disorders, difficulties during sexual interaction, erectile dysfunction, dysfunctions of desire, inability to achieve an orgasm, seductive behaviors, uncontrollable sexual activity, advanced sexual behavior; confusion of sexuality (gender) and relationship problems.

I rebuke seasonal, chronic and prolonged illnesses tied to Jezebel's witchcraft.

I rebuke strange and regular accidents or injuries.

I rebuke all emotional and psychological deprivation in my life.

I rebuke the spirit of rejection of self and by others that I picked up in the womb.

I rebuke the spirit of abandonment from my biological father and/or mother.

I rebuke the spirit of nakedness that came from the loss of spiritual and physical protection from my parents, church and government leaders.

I take authority over and rebuke all controlling spirits released against me from my mother and render them powerless, in the name of Jesus.

I rebuke the passive-aggressive personality prescribed by Jezebel for her victims.

I rebuke the black widow spider seduction of Jezebel and choose to no longer remain entangled in her web of carnage.

# Renunciations

A **'renunciation'** is an act or instance of relinquishing, abandoning, repudiating, or sacrificing something, as a right, title, person, or ambition. Self-renunciation is the act of renouncing, sacrificing or giving up or surrendering a possession or right or title or privilege etc.

Words associated with renunciation are: denial, refusal, relinquishment, resignation and surrender.

Renunciation is one of the most powerful tools that a believer can use to free themself from Jezebel's sorceries and witchcrafts. In my many years of deliverance ministry, I have found that when a person begins to renounce all relations with Jezebelic networks, (allegiance to her will, alliances and agreements made through demonic people, places or things associated with her network) that there is an immediate lifting of demonic oppression and increased mental and emotional clarity.

As you begin the renunciation process you are effectively coming out of agreement with Jezebel's plans, purpose and direction for your life. Renouncing Jezebel is letting her know that you reject her claim to your mind, will and emotions.

Renouncing Jezebel and her network is **YOU** taking authority. As you begin to pray these prayers of renunciations against Jezebel and her incantations, you are letting that spirit know you disown and reject it. You are boldly stating that you no longer belong to anything tied to Jezebel. Renouncing Jezebel informs her that you have resigned from any partnership with her and no longer have any allegiance, obligation or duty to her network.

Remember the spirit of Jezebel considers her host her property. Over the years, Jezebel's cunning craftiness may have tricked you into coming into agreement with her ways. Whether you knew it or not, Jezebel set you up to do her bidding. Your behaviors, actions, communication and thoughts were motivated by her influence on your life. Through her deception she employed your life to enlarge her evil network. Perhaps you've been a victim of Jezebel's witchcraft and find yourself in a state of hopelessness, frustration and despair. It's time to break free through the renunciation process.

As you go through the process of verbally renouncing the spirit of Jezebel, you may begin to experience a lifting of the heaviness and weight from Jezebel's domination over your life. As her oppression begins to lift off you, continue to press as a warrior determined to root out every area that Jezebel gained a stronghold in.

To renounce is to deny. Begin to deny Jezebel any rights into your life ever again.

*Teaching us that, denying ungodliness and worldly lusts, we should live soberly, righteously, and godly, in this present world – Titus 2:12*

---

Heavenly Father, I ask for your forgiveness for being an enabler to the spirit of Jezebel. I have tolerated her ways and she has controlled my life long enough. I confess that I was in agreement and compliance with her network, whether willingly or ignorantly, I received her deceptive tricks and got caught in her web of destruction.

Heavenly Father, I renounce my relationship with the spirit of Jezebel, and ask that her demonic infiltration in all parts of my mind, will, emotion and body be rooted out until nothing remains.

I reject, revoke and renounce my involvement to and with any of the following evil activities and associations tied to the Jezebel spirit. The occult, Ouija boards, Charlie-Charlie, sorcery, mind-control (witchcraft), Wicca, black magic, voodoo, divination, fortune-telling, talking to demons, handwriting analysis, crystal balls, tarot cards, palm readings, astrology, horoscope, fascination with the signs of the zodiac, hypnosis, spiritualism, séances, bewitchments, enchantments, conjurations, incantations, necromancy, clairvoyance, transcendental meditation, soul travel, carnal prayers, powders, candles, incense, touch stones, power objects, the kabbalah, third eye, curses of sickness and disease and all marriage breaking curses.

I renounce all association with Eastern religion, Hinduism, Confucianism, Zen, Jehovah witnesses, Christian science, Mormonism, Baptist, Methodist, Lutheran, Pentecostal, Episcopalian, Roman Catholicism, Lutheran, Apostolic Faith, COGIC, Unity, Scientology, religious hate groups, terrorism, racial groups including White supremacy groups, Aryan brotherhood, Zionism, KKK, Black panthers, Black Muslims and any other religious denomination or sect.

I confess the following iniquities on behalf of myself, my ancestors (from both sides of my family) and receive emancipation from Jezebel's network. I renounce and cast down all agreement, confederacy, alliance and form of rebellion, whoredom, perversion, pride, witchcraft, evil communication, covenant breaking, lust, fornication, homosexuality, lesbianism, incest, rape, other forms of sexual uncleanness, and domination including prostitution, masturbation, pornography, sexting and adultery.

I renounce religious associations, carrying the message of witches and warlocks (witchcraft), false motives and hidden agendas.

I renounce allegiance to Jezebel's kingdom and every occasion in which I walked away from the Kingdom of God and returned to the kingdom of darkness.

I renounce every form of idol worship, causing the land, which I live in to be contaminated.

I renounce taking advantage of every opportunity to be in a photograph with church leaders and VIP's in order to give the appearance that I am 'special' or 'connected' to that person.

I renounce name-dropping and fabricating stories about people that I do not know or have never met.

I repent of and renounce all worship at the altars of Baal in my family line. I declare that my household and I are coming out of that kingdom in Jesus' name.

Father, in the name of Jesus I repent from being used as a host for the Jezebel spirit. Forgive me for my association with her network, eunuchs and children. I renounce all idolatry, lusts of the flesh and areas of rebellion.

I renounce every form of bloodshed upon the land I have lived, including murder, gossip, slander, whispering and lying.

I renounce and repent of operating with a mocking spirit, making fun of people, making light of serious concerns, issues, situations and people.

I renounce, break and loose myself from all Jezebelic subjection to my mother, father, grandparents, or any human being, living or dead, who has dominated me in any way.

I renounce the hatred and despising of women.

I renounce the hatred and despising of men.

I renounce all un-forgiveness and bitterness towards my biological father and mother.

I renounce all un-forgiveness and bitterness towards those that are deceased and in the grave.

I renounce and repent of being a controlling man, woman, husband, wife or child.

I renounce being an arrogant, prideful, untouchable, un-teachable, un-reachable and stubborn leader.

I renounce (as a leader) all forms of manipulation, control and perversion against the flock of God.

I renounce the worship of Molech by sacrificing my children through abortion, neglect, abandonment, abuse and selfishness.

I renounce every form of spiritual whoredom, harlotry and idolatry.

I renounce being a recruiter for Jezebel and carrying her message of witchcraft, false motives, hidden agendas and religious ideologies.

I renounce the spirit of racism as a result of attending one of Jezebel's religious indoctrination centers.

I renounce the spirit of religious deception whereby Jezebel kept me ignorant of the Kingdom of God through focusing on religious order, protocol, activities and by-laws.

I renounce giving the spirit of Whoredoms permission to cause me to walk in error or influenced me to come under the authority, rule, reign and domination of the spirit of idolatry and entertainment operating in the religious culture.

I renounce Jezebel's erroneous doctrines, mindsets, attitudes and wickedness.

I renounce all rebellion, pride, arrogance, control and manipulation I've had towards the five ascension gifts and my leaders.

I renounce all disrespect, slander and gossip I've operated in towards by brothers and sister in the Lord and leaders that watched over my soul.

I renounce all prayers of witchcraft I've released in the name of 'intercession' and 'concern.'

I renounce being tolerant of the Jezebel spirit in my home, my church and my community.

I renounce the fear, intimidation and torment of Jezebel.

I renounce passivity and terror that has prohibited me from confronting those who are or have operated with a Jezebel spirit.

I renounce my compliance to Jezebelic leaders, ministries, churches and organizations.

I renounce my association and involvement with Jezebelic [religious], denominations and networks.

I renounce every tie to Jezebel's nature of rebellion, independence and hatred of men and Godly authority.

I renounce and break every link to Jezebel's nature of pride and rebellion that has blocked me from communicating, sharing, giving and collaborating with others.

I renounce all ungodly alliance with Jezebel and come into total alignment with the Spirit of God, the Kingdom of Heaven, the government of God and the ruler-ship of the Lord Jesus Christ in my life.

I renounce my fixation with being in-charge and in control of everything and everyone I come in contact with.

I renounce talkativeness and the need to have the last word.

I renounce the use of false authority through name dropping and lying.

I renounce and break every effect of the suffering and sorrow from the stronghold of Jezebel, queen of heaven.

I renounce self-idolatry, self-indulgence, self-promotion, self-exaltation and self-pity associated with the Jezebel spirit.

I renounce all selfish ambitions, self-gratification, self-justification and my desire to please man more than the Lord Jesus Christ.

I renounce the false kingdom of Jezebel and come out of agreement with the 'queen of heaven' and her religious network.

I renounce all covetousness and desire towards those in positions of authority, specifically in the church, ministry or workplace.

I renounce all ungodly independence and come into total dependence upon the Lord, His word and the voice of the Holy Spirit.

I repent of and renounce every obsession to rule and be in control, where the principality of Jezebel has been given rights by my ancestors.

I renounce and break every effect of the suffering and sorrow of the stronghold of Jezebel.

I renounce and break the self-idolatry, self-indulgence, self-pity, self-promotion and exaltation of the Jezebel spirit.

I renounce and break every effect of the garments and royal robes of the harlot Jezebel.

I renounce being a spokesperson for Jezebel in my church, against the people of God, against family members, business associates, friends and strangers.

I repent of indecisiveness and choose to come into Godly obedience, submission and fully surrender myself to the purpose, plan and will of God for my life.

I renounce and break the Jezebelic sword (word) of division. I break it off my life, my family and my church in Jesus' name.

I renounce and break every tie to Jezebel the 'mother of harlots' through seduction and sexual sin in my family line.

I renounce all affluence, power, position, titles, status and riches I received through ungodly ways specifically tied to Jezebel, such as control, manipulation and [sexual] seduction.

I renounce all corporate and political power and ungodly financial gain received by deploying Jezebelic tactics.

I renounce and break every curse of fornication, prostitution, perversion and occult sex off my life in Jesus' name.

I renounce false crying, pouting and self-pity.

I renounce the drama queen spirit that had me put on a show to gain attention.

I renounce all inferiority and low self-esteem I had due to receiving the lies of Jezebel.

I renounce the spirit of perfectionism operating in my life.

I renounce the usage of drugs, alcohol, plants, seeds, and roots for the purpose of intoxication, getting high, drunk and loss of control of my mental and physical faculties.

I renounce my association and involvement in participating in the fasting of Jezebel. (1 Kings 21:9)

I renounce the spirit of withdrawal and wandering that come from Jezebels attacks.

I renounce and break every curse of the loss of children, whether emotional or physical.

I renounce and break every curse of being a widow, husbandless, even within marriage, and without headship to protect and guard my physical and emotional life.

I renounce the stronghold of deception that comes with the kingdom of Jezebel.

I repent of and renounce all Jezebelic attitudes and manifestations including: jealousy, envy, arrogance pride, fear, lust, covetousness, permissiveness, accusation, divisiveness, lying, disloyalty, bitterness, rage, self doubt, rebelliousness, discouragement, confusion, extreme feminism, hatred of male authority, fault finding, temper tantrums, criticism and manipulation.

I renounce all sexual perversions and immorality tied to Jezebel including: adultery, orgies, fornication, lust, unclean thoughts, perversions, oral sex, anal sex, homosexuality, lesbianism, incest, compulsive and chronic masturbation, harlotry and pornography.

I renounce Jezebel's religious abnormalities including (but not limited to): idolatry, divisions, fractions and sects in the Church, apostasy, heresies, spiritual blindness, false worship, false tongues, false laying on of hands, false prophetic, false apostolic, false salvation, false deliverance, religious spirits, blasphemy and secular humanism.

I renounce all association and involvement with the Kundalini spirit and Jezebel's mind control including: uncontrollable physical sensations such as crying, laughing, jerking, shaking, twitching, barking, strange animal noises, falling down, rolling around the floor (as if drunk) and New Age soaking.

## Binding, Breaking, Cutting & Loosing

While the terms **"binding"** and **"loosing"** have been somewhat abused in Christianity, specifically among groups that believe in spiritual warfare and deliverance, there is a place for it when contending with the spirit of Jezebel. In it's simplest and purest forms; to "bind" is to forbid, and to "loose" is to permit.

To bind and loose is the authority to declare what is God's mind on a matter of doctrine or practice. To "bind" is to force, compel, make or require. The authority to "bind" is only valid when used in submission to Christ's word or teaching. It does not give the church the authority to develop or engage in esoteric teachings or practices. Therefore when "binding" one must make certain that they are submitted to God and not simply going through a religious exercise.

*And I will give unto thee the keys of the kingdom of heaven: and whatsoever thou shalt **bind** on earth shall be bound in heaven: and whatsoever thou shalt **loose** on earth shall be loosed in heaven – Matthew 16:19*

To bind means to: confine, restrain, restrict and constrain with legal authority.

When contending with Jezebel's witchcrafts, binding is the application of taking the responsibility to stop her from further carnage in your life.

**Breaking** and **cutting** are terms used in deliverance ministry and when engaged in warfare prayers, they are very effective terms when receiving deliverance from Jezebel in your personal life.

To break means to: separate into parts or pieces often in a sudden and forceful or violent way. To cut is to: divide into parts and to separate.

*But ye shall destroy their altars, break their images, and cut down their groves: For thou shalt worship no other god: for the Lord, whose name is Jealous, is a jealous God – Exodus 34:13-14*

Binding, breaking, cutting and destroying the effects of Jezebel against your soul is a forceful way of verbalizing your Kingdom authority and root out the altars of idolatry, perversion and witchcrafts that you or your ancestors have erected. As Kingdom citizens, you are called to remove obstacles in your life that hinder and oppose.

*See, I have this day set thee over the nations and over the kingdoms, to root out, and to pull down, and to destroy, and to throw down, to build, and to plant – Jeremiah 1:10*

Family curses can be destroyed through alignment and agreement with Christ's redeeming work at Calvary. As you begin to break the curse of Jezebel, you do so with the authority of Jesus Christ, and by the power of the Holy Spirit.

*Christ hath redeemed us from the curse of the law, being made a curse for us: for it is written, Cursed is every one that hangeth on a tree – Galatians 3:14*

*Behold, I give unto you power to tread on serpents and scorpions, and over all the power of the enemy: and nothing shall by any means hurt you – Luke 10:19*

*And these signs shall follow them that believe; In my name shall they cast out devils; they shall speak with new tongues; They shall take up serpents; and if they drink any deadly thing, it shall not hurt them; they shall lay hands on the sick, and they shall recover – Mark 16: 17-18*

*But ye shall receive power, after that the Holy Ghost is come upon you – Acts 1:8 (a)*

---

I bind and sever the five-fold cord of Jezebel; Religion, witchcraft, perversion, compromise and idolatry.

I bind spirits of passivity and tolerance towards Jezebel, her eunuchs and prophets.

I bind the spirit of Herodias and cut off all retaliation spirits released against me for exposing Jezebel, her network, whoredoms and perversion. (Mark 6:22-24).

I bind, sever and break evil spirits of charismatic witchcraft released against me through controlling prayers and prophetic sorcery.

I bind every spirit of fear that has come in through the womb. I break its hold and command it to loose me in Jesus' name.

I bind all headaches and pain associated with witchcraft, hexes, spells, voodoo, Christian word curses, fatigue, allergies, tiredness, stress, sickness, Leviathan, Python, Marine demons, Jezebel Networks, retaliation, assassinating demons, squid mind binding demons, soul ties and ungodly agreements in Jesus name.

I bind all psychic attacks, assignments, operations, deposits, mechanisms, activities, blueprints, plots, plans, designs, traps, wiles, snares, curses, hexes, vexes, bewitchments, enchantments, cords, and judgments of Jezebel, in Jesus name.

I bind the spirit of death that plagues my family. I break all associations and covenants with death and destruction made by my forefathers from the nations that my ancestors came from.

I take authority over the retaliation of Jezebel and bind the murdering spirit, the hoodlum spirit, bopper spirits, gangbanging spirits and violence from operating in my life.

I bind all emotional hurts, deep wounds and trauma I've experienced in life from controlling Jezebels that left me in a catatonic state of denial, deception, delusion and despair.

I bind Jezebel's retaliatory posture that has me isolate myself from touch, and the inability to give or receive love.

I bind all retaliatory curses of Jezebel that bring rejection, abandonment, fear, laziness, insecurity, idleness, passivity, neglect and despair.

I bind and take authority over all retaliatory curses from Jezebel against church growth, discipleship and outreach to new converts and members.

I bind all retaliatory curses from Jezebel against my home, family, children, my job, businesses, transportation, employment, finances, church property and equipment, all curses over the finances of the church (gifts, tithes, offerings, pledges), all curses causing visitors to never return and legacy members to leave, curses against the prayer ministry of the church, all curses against praise and worship, against teaching sound doctrine and preaching the Kingdom of God.

I bind all retaliatory curses from Jezebel against deliverance ministry, impartation and activation of the gifts of the Holy Spirit, healings and receiving sound doctrine.

I bind all retaliatory curses from Jezebel causing disunity, pride, rebellion, strife, gossip, criticism, and confusion. All curses causing jealousy, envy, selfishness and competition among church members and the leadership team, leave now in Jesus name.

I bind all retaliatory curses from Jezebel against the intercessory prayer ministry and the hospitality ministry of the church preventing the members from praying, interceding and serving the body of Christ.

I bind all retaliatory curses from Jezebel causing fear, phobia, paranoia, worry, apprehension, and nervousness against engaging in spiritual warfare.

I bind the following curses associated with Jezebel and her network as a result of my personal involvement or my ancestors' with her witchcrafts and activities:

- Curse of the automatic failure syndrome
- Curse of poverty and lack

- Curse of suffering
- Curse of downheartedness and despair
- Curse of judgment
- Curse of death
- Curse of humiliation
- Curse of nakedness
- Curse of slavery and bondage
- Curse of senility
- Curse of madness
- Curse of homosexuality and lesbianism
- Curse of cancer
- Curse of an unstable mind
- Curse of schizophrenia
- Curse of divorce
- Curse of male & female domination
- Curse of incest and rape
- Curse of the womb (loss of children)
- Curse of losing marriage partner
- Curse of disasters and evil
- Curse of loneliness and desolation
- Curse of witchcraft
- Curse of discrimination
- Curse of racism
- Curse of illiteracy
- Curse of murder
- Curse of violence

I break the spirit of control that binds me to take control of others.

I break the root of iniquity from off my life.

I break every soul tie to the mystery of injustice, wickedness and darkness.

I break the curse of death spoken against my friends and church family.

I break curses of death spoken against families in my region, and in my nation.

I break every word curse of death spoken out of the mouth of believers.

I break, cut and saw asunder the spirit of suicide; I take authority over every evil work that looks to bring terror by night.

I break every effect of the throne and the authority of the Jezebel in my life and my family.

I break all idolatry of men in my family.

I break the idolatry of the women in my family.

I break the tie to physical incest.

I break every unhealthy or perverted tie to my mother or any other mother figure in my life.

I break the tie to spiritual incest.

I break every unhealthy or perverted tie to my spiritual father, covering authority or any other father figure in my life that I looked to that would fill the void of not having my biological father in my life.

I break the stronghold of Jezebel that emasculates the men in my family, keeping them immature, passive and in need of a mother to support and care for them.

I break every spell and incantation put upon me from former lovers that joined in Jezebels perversions.

I break off of my body every generational curse of cancer that has come through Jezebel's attack against my life or my partnership with her.

I break Jezebel's witchcraft, whoredoms and perversions off every part of my mind, will and emotions; my conscious and unconscious; off my body and soul, my finances, my marriage my posterity, my present and my future.

I break the effects of rejection by Christian brothers, sisters, pastors and leaders.

I break every covenant with Jezebel entered into by my parents, grandparents or great-grand parents, on my behalf and all the oppression that comes with it.

I break the power, manipulation, lies, denial, and deception caused by the spirit of Jezebel.

I break the powers of every word curse and witchcraft spoken against my life by Jezebel.

I break every demon spirit associated with car fatalities, including road rage, alcoholic and drug usage.

I break all generational curses that bring premature death, including death in the womb, infant death, childhood death, adolescent death, and death before the age of 100 (Is 65:20).

I cut off the assignment of Jezebel against the servants of the Kingdom (1 Kings 19:2).

I remove myself from Jezebels table and cut off its sustenance supply (1 Kings 18:19).

I sever the cord of Jezebel's false religion and her seat of false authority operating in my life.

I cut the cord of occult powers between Jezebel and her seat of false authority operating in my life.

I cut every cord attached to Jezebel's throne and annihilate every consequence of being attached to that throne in my life in the name of Jesus.

I cut the cord of woman-dominated ruler-ship and government.

I cut off the assignment of Jezebel and her children against my family, my church, my business and my life.

I sever the cord of compromise, tolerance and passivity that I've had towards Jezebel and her children.

I detached the Jezebel spirit from operating in my life, ministry, church, business and marriage. I break the curse of Jezebel back to ten generations on both sides of the family. I cut, sever, break and destroy all cords, snares, fetters, chains and weapons of control used by this evil network.

I cut off the assignment of Jezebel against my finances and investments.

I cut and sever every spiritual cord that binds me to Jezebel's kingdom and I declare I am coming out of the religious system of the harlot woman of Revelation.

I sever all ties with the sorceress Jezebel and remove all witchcraft out of her hand. Jezebel you will no longer cast spells on me (Micah 5:12).

I detach from Jezebel's web and close every portal, gate access point, door and entrance in and around my life right now, in Jesus name.

As a grown adult, I sever the mother-child relationship and command all Jezebelic patterns to be broken.

I sever the relationship to Jezebel's bedchamber and remove myself from her den of lust, perversion and debauchery.

I loose persecution against the kingdom of Jezebel (Rev. 2:22).

I loose myself from the blasphemies of Jezebel.

I loose myself from all curses of the spirit of Jezebel operating in my bloodline. I break every curse associated with being in Jezebels bedchamber including discouragement, death, humiliation, nakedness, slavery, senility, homosexuality and lesbianism, cancer, schizophrenia, divorce, female domination, male domination, incest, loss of children, loss of spouse, disasters, accidents, loneliness, desolation and financial ruin.

I root out all division and confusion out of my marriage and release the spirit of unity into my marriage.

I smash the Jezebelic religious government off my life.

**Other Books by Apostle Robert Summers**

Deliverance Training Manual ©

It's about Time

Genuine Fathers – Willing Sons ©

Kingdom Principles of Success, Wealth & Prosperity ©

Harboring the Spirit of Jezebel ©

Gossip – The Weapon of Mass Destruction ©


For a complete listing of resources please visit www.summersministries.com

Made in the USA
San Bernardino, CA
29 November 2019